# Join in with us!
# LETTERS

by Karen O'Callaghan

Illustrated by Eric Rowe

Brimax Books · Cambridge · England

ISBN 0 86112 125 2
All rights reserved
© Brimax Rights Ltd. 1982
Published by Brimax Books
Cambridge England 1982
Printed in Belgium

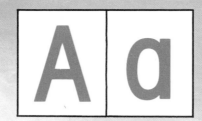

# A a

Alex is looking all around for Zoe.

"Here I am, Alex!"

Point to all the Aa's.

# B b

Blow a piece of paper across the floor.
Bend down low and

blow, blow and blow!

Where are the Bb's ?

# C c

Curl up tight,
make yourself smaller.

Can you curl up too?

Can you see the Cc's?

# D d

Dancing is fun!

You can do it too!

Alex dances
with teddy

Zoe makes the doll
dance as well!

Where are the Dd's?

# E e

Eating ice cream...

Alex is still
eating his
ice cream.

"Mine's all gone,"
says Zoe.
"Now it's empty."

Can you see the Ee's?

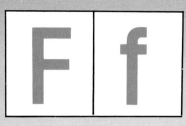

# F f

Finding the best way...
"These won't fit in," says Alex.

"If we fold them they will fit," says Zoe.
"Folding makes things smaller."

Fold a piece of paper.
Does it get smaller?

Find all the Ff's.

# G g

"Go on Zoe, open it!" says Alex.

Who is getting
a present?

Who is giving
a present?

Where are all the Gg's?

# H h

Here is Alex holding a box.

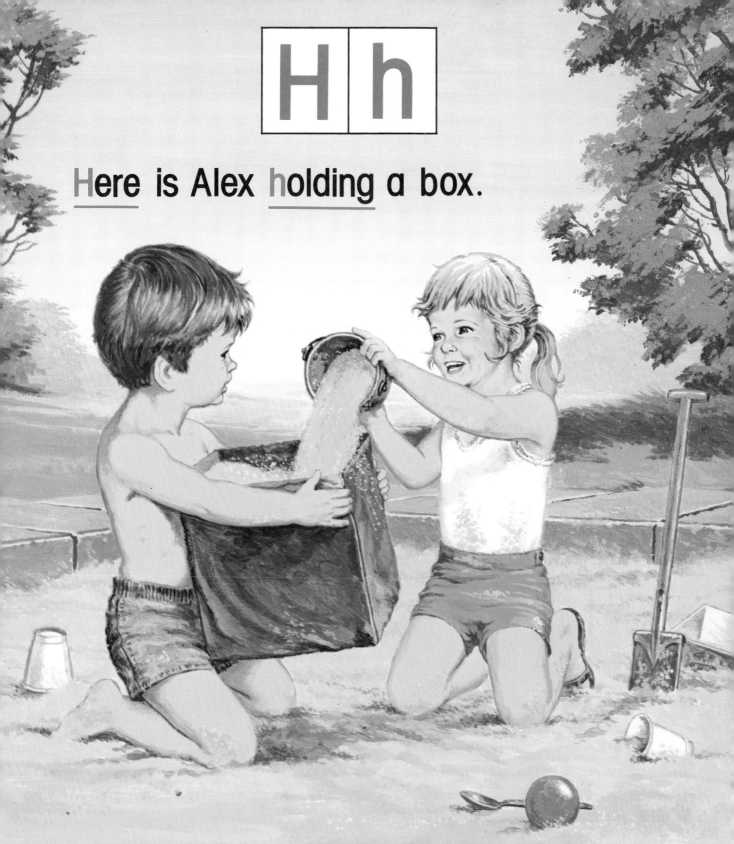

Zoe is helping him to fill it with sand.

How many Hh's are there ?

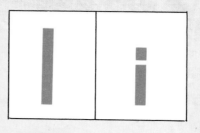

"_I_ am _insi_de our tent," says Zoe.

"_I_ am _i_ns_i_de _i_t too," says Alex.

F_i_nd the _Ii_'s

# J j

Join in a jumping game!

Just jump a little -
and you're there!

Point to the J j's

# K k

Kick a ball as hard as you can,
see how far it goes!

Look, Alex kicks the leaves
up in the air and everywhere.

Look for all the Kk's

# L l

Look at Alex, he is trying to lift the bricks all at once.

Zoe can't do it - she is laughing!

Look for all the Ll's

# Mm

Moving about...

"I can see myself
in the mirror."

"When I move,
my shadow moves with me."

How many Mm's can you find ?

# Nn

Nod your head to mean 'Yes'...

up

and

down

Now shake your head
from side to side to mean 'No'.

Point to the Nn's

# O o

"Over the chairs we go!"

"We climb on — and jump off!"

Point to the Oo's.

# P p

"Please help me, Zoe.
We can move this together!"

"I'll push."

"I'll pull."

Point to the Pp's

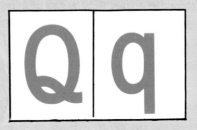

# Q q

Quiet! Shh! Shh!

Sit quietly.

What can you hear
when you don't make a noise?

Where is the Q and q?

# R r

Run, run as fast as you can.

Round and round and round!

Find the Rr's.

# S s

See us sharing something.

"One for you and one for me –
one for you and one for me."

Spot the S's 's

# T t

Touch some hing rough like tree bark.

Look for something smooth to touch
like flower petals.

Touch all the Tt's

# U u

"Under we go!"

You must make yourself flat
to go under the chairs.

Can you find the Uu's?

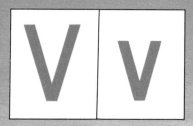

**Vv**

Visiting is fun!

Zoe is going to visit Alex.

Alex wa<u>v</u>es, he is
<u>v</u>ery pleased to see Zoe.

Where is the <u>V</u> and <u>v</u>?

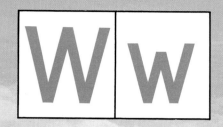

# W w

Walking two ways!
Walk with great big steps.

Walk with tiny little steps.

Where are the Ww's?

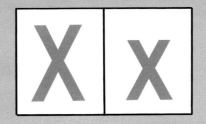

# X x

It's e<u>x</u>citing making <u>X</u>'s!

Make yourself look like an <u>X</u>.

Make e<u>x</u>tra <u>X</u>'s with legs and fingers.

Spot the <u>X</u><u>x</u>'s

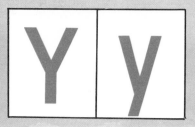

"You're yawning, Alex," says Zoe.
"I can see you!"

"I'm not tired," says Alex.

"Come and play."

How many Yy's can you see?

# Z z

Zoe and Alex are following

a zigzag path.

"Goodbye!"

Point to each letter Z.